GREEN ANACONDAS

BY EMILY ROSE OACHS

BELLWETHER MEDIA • MINNEAPOLIS, MN

EPIC

EPIC BOOKS are no ordinary books. They burst with intense action, high-speed heroics, and shadows of the unknown. Are you ready for an Epic adventure?

This edition first published in 2014 by Bellwether Media, Inc.

Library of Congress Cataloging-in-Publication Data

Oachs, Emily Rose, author.
 Green Anacondas / by Emily Rose Oachs.
    pages cm. – (Epic. Amazing Snakes!)
  Summary: "Engaging images accompany information about green anacondas. The combination of high-interest subject matter and light text is intended for students in grades 2 through 7"– Provided by publisher.
  Audience: Ages 7-12.
  Includes bibliographical references and index.
  ISBN 978-1-62617-093-3 (hardcover : alk. paper)
  1. Anaconda–Juvenile literature. I. Title.
  QL666.O63O234 2014
  597.96'7–dc23
                    2013036624

Printed in the United States of America, North Mankato, MN.

TABLE OF CONTENTS

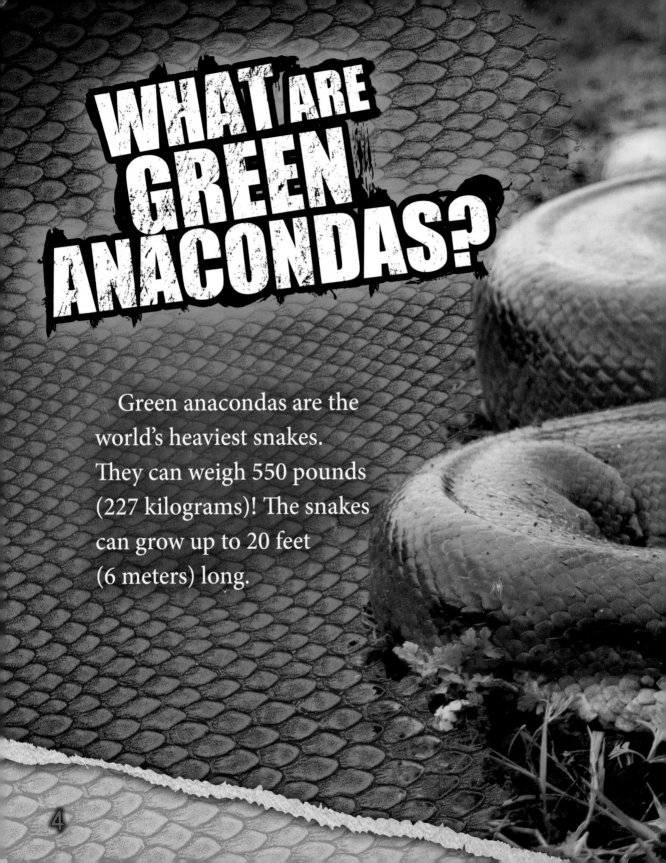

WHAT ARE GREEN ANACONDAS?

Green anacondas are the world's heaviest snakes. They can weigh 550 pounds (227 kilograms)! The snakes can grow up to 20 feet (6 meters) long.

5

Olive green **scales** cover their bodies. They also have black, brown, and yellow spots. These colors **camouflage** the anacondas.

WHERE GREEN ANACONDAS LIVE

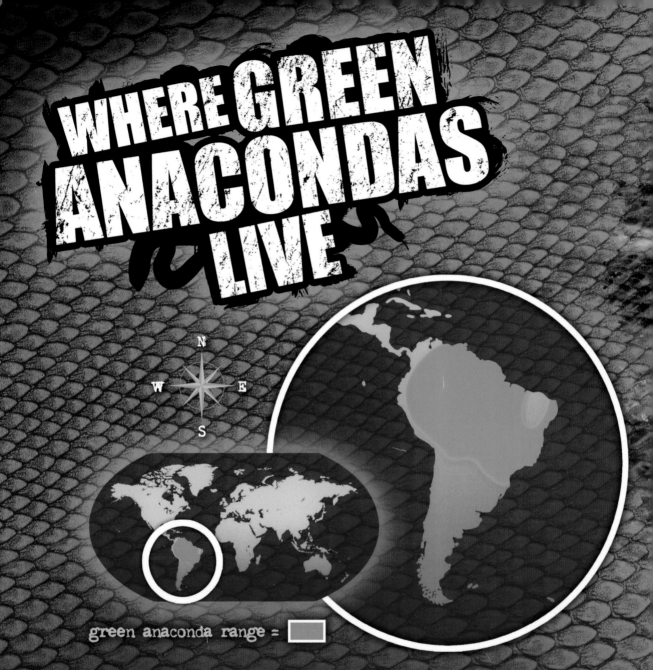

N
W   E
S

green anaconda range =

Green anacondas are found in **tropical** parts of South America. They live near the swamps and streams of **rain forests** and **savannahs**.

Buried Alive

During dry seasons, green anacondas bury themselves in the mud. They can stay there for months before rain falls again!

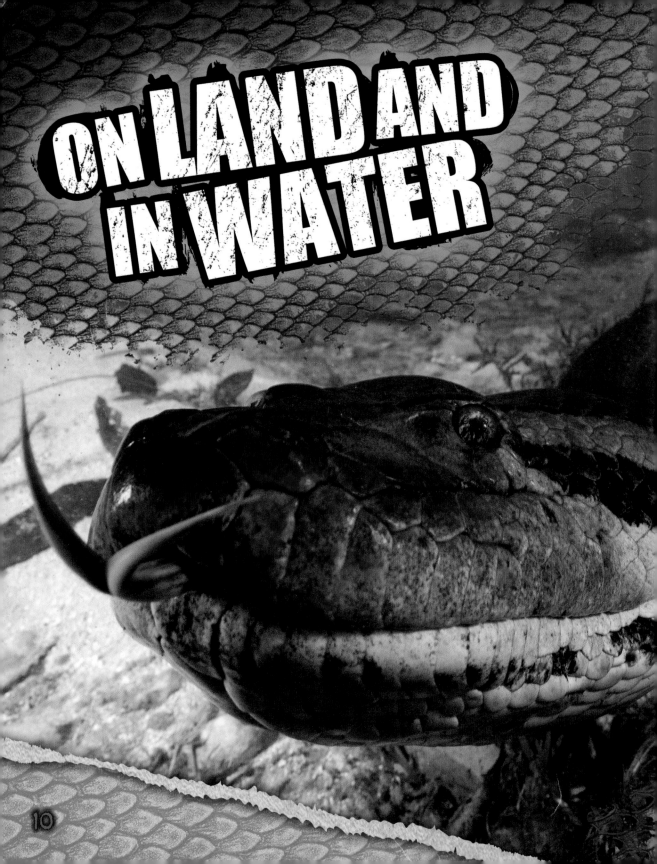

ON LAND AND IN WATER

Green anacondas spend most of their lives around water. They are powerful swimmers. Their speed in the water makes them dangerous hunters.

HUNTING FOR PREY

Killer Name

Green anacondas have also been called "bull killers."

**Green
Anaconda
Prey**

Green anacondas hunt for **prey** at night.
They wait in murky water for birds, fish,
deer, and other animals to come close.

13

Then green anacondas attack.
Their curved teeth hold prey.
The snakes **coil** around their
meal and squeeze tightly.

No Breathing Room
Sometimes green anacondas
drown animals in water to
kill them.

Green anacondas have stretchy jaws. These allow the snakes to open their mouths wide. Then the anacondas slowly swallow animals in one piece.

Jaguars and caimans sometimes hunt these massive snakes. Green anacondas do not have many other **predators**. Few animals are large enough to attack them!

Hunter or Hunted?

Green anacondas also hunt jaguars and caimans.

SPECIES PROFILE

SCIENTIFIC NAME: *EUNECTES MURINUS*

NICKNAME: WATER BOA

AVERAGE SIZE: 20 FEET (6 METERS)

HABITATS: RAIN FORESTS, SAVANNAHS

COUNTRIES: ARGENTINA, BOLIVIA, BRAZIL, COLOMBIA, ECUADOR, FRENCH GUINEA, GUYANA, PARAGUAY, PERU, SURINAME, TRINIDAD AND TOBAGO

VENOMOUS: NO

HUNTING METHOD: CONSTRICTION

COMMON PREY: BIRDS, CAIMANS, CAPYBARAS, DEER, FISH, TAPIRS, PIGS, TURTLES, JAGUARS

GLOSSARY

camouflage—to hide an animal or thing by helping it blend in with the surroundings

coil—to wrap around

predators—animals that hunt other animals for food

prey—animals that are hunted by other animals for food

rain forests—hot, rainy areas with tall trees

savannahs—flat, grassy land with few trees

scales—small plates of skin that cover and protect a snake's body

tropical—part of a hot, rainy region near the equator

TO LEARN MORE

At the Library

Krebs, Laurie. *We're Roaming in the Rainforest: An Amazon Adventure*. Cambridge, Mass.: Barefoot Books, 2010.

Lynette, Rachel. *Anacondas*. New York, N.Y.: PowerKids Press, 2013.

Sexton, Colleen. *Anacondas*. Minneapolis, Minn.: Bellwether Media, 2010.

On the Web

Learning more about green anacondas is as easy as 1, 2, 3.

1. Go to www.factsurfer.com.

2. Enter "green anacondas" into the search box.

3. Click the "Surf" button and you will see a list of related Web sites.

With factsurfer.com, finding more information is just a click away.

INDEX